D1611965

DEC   2012

Sea Turtle Hatchlings

by Ruth Owen

Consultant:
Therese Conant
NOAA Fisheries
Office of Protected Resources
Silver Spring, Maryland

BEARPORT
PUBLISHING

New York, New York

Credits

Cover, © Mark Conlin VWPics/SuperStock; 4–5, ©Khoroshunova Olga/Shutterstock (background); 5, ©Wild Wonders of Europe/Zankl/Nature Picture Library (turtle); 6, ©Cosmographics; 7, ©Peter Leahy/Shutterstock; 9, ©Lynda Richardson/Corbis; 10, ©Minden Pictures/Superstock; 11, ©Doug Perrine/Seapics.com; 12–13, ©Ann & Steve Toon/Nature Picture Library; 14–15, ©Lynda Richardson/Corbis; 16–17, ©Lynda Richardson/Corbis; 19TL, ©Andaman/Shutterstock; 19TR, ©Nastya Pirieva/Shutterstock; 19B, ©Doug Perrine/Seapics.com; 20–21, ©Luiz Claudio Marigo/Nature Picture Library; 22T, ©Peter Leahy/Shutterstock; 22B, ©Minden Pictures/Superstock; 23T, ©Ann & Steve Toon/Nature Picture Library; 23C, ©Lynda Richardson/Corbis; 23B, ©Natalie Jean/Shutterstock.

Publisher: Kenn Goin
Senior Editor: Lisa Wiseman
Creative Director: Spencer Brinker
Design: Emma Randall
Editor: Mark J Sachner
Photo Researcher: Ruby Tuesday Books Ltd

Library of Congress Cataloging-in-Publication Data

Owen, Ruth, 1967–
 Sea turtle hatchlings / By Ruth Owen.
  p. cm. — (Water babies)
 Includes bibliographical references and index.
 ISBN 978-1-61772-603-3 (library binding) — ISBN 1-61772-603-6 (library binding)
 1. Sea turtles—Infancy—Juvenile literature. I. Title.
 QL666.C536O94 2013
 597.92'8139—dc23
                            2012012881

For more information, write to Bearport Publishing Company, Inc., 45 West 21st Street, Suite 3B, New York, New York 10010. Printed in the United States of America.

10 9 8 7 6 5 4 3 2 1

Contents

A very special night

It is nighttime on a warm, sandy beach.

Suddenly, a tiny head and two **flippers** appear from under the sand.

It's a baby loggerhead turtle.

The tiny turtle is leaving its underground **nest**.

Tonight is the start of a big adventure!

What is a loggerhead turtle?

A loggerhead turtle is a large animal that lives in warm oceans.

An adult turtle can weigh as much as seven children.

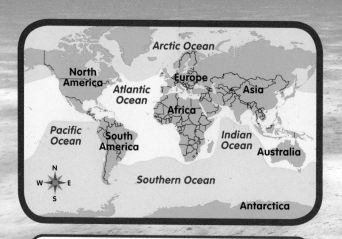

Arctic Ocean

North America

Europe

Atlantic Ocean

Asia

Africa

Pacific Ocean

South America

Indian Ocean

Australia

N
W   E
S

Southern Ocean

Antarctica

Where loggerhead turtles live

A loggerhead turtle has four flippers that it uses to help it swim.

It also has a thick shell that helps protect it from enemies.

flipper

shell

Adult loggerhead turtle size

A turtle nest

A female loggerhead turtle lays her eggs in the spring or summer.

She swims to the shore and crawls from the ocean onto the beach.

Then, she uses her flippers to dig a deep hole in the sand.

In the hole, which is her nest, she lays up to 120 eggs.

Then she covers the eggs with sand.

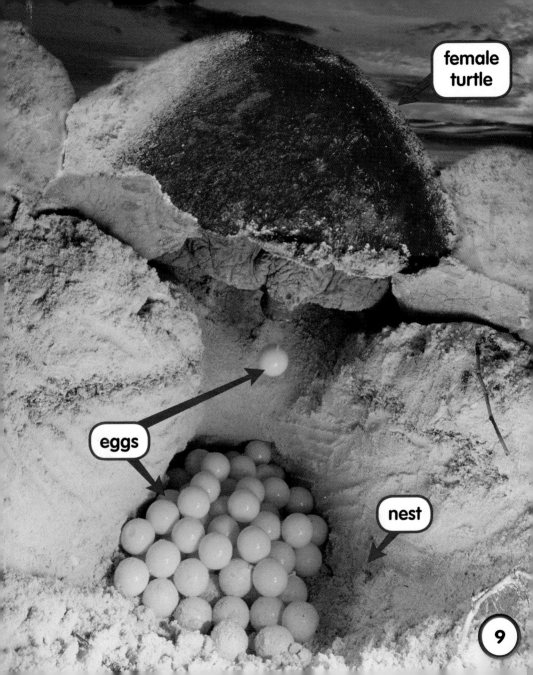

female turtle

eggs

nest

9

The baby turtles hatch

A mother turtle doesn't take care of her eggs or her babies.

After she's hidden her nest in the sand, she crawls back to the ocean.

About six weeks later, the baby turtles begin to **hatch** from their eggs.

baby turtle hatching

egg

Once every tiny turtle has hatched, they dig their way up through the sand.

They will not go out onto the beach until it is nighttime.

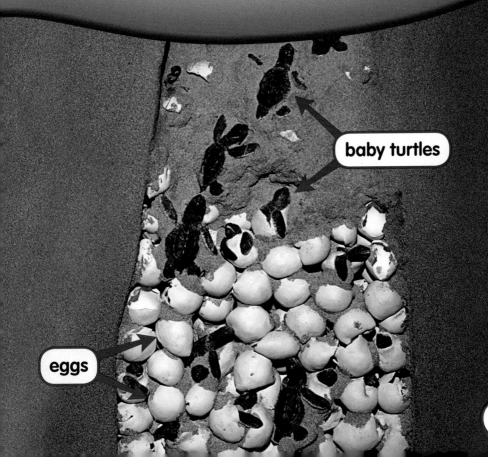

baby turtles

eggs

A dangerous time

Once it gets dark, the turtle **hatchlings** dig their way out onto the beach.

This is a very dangerous time for the tiny turtles.

Seabirds and crabs may be waiting on the beach to eat them.

The tiny turtles must run to the ocean before they are caught.

hatchlings

Run, hatchlings, run!

Each tiny turtle runs as fast as it can over the sand.

The turtle hatchlings have no parent to lead them to the ocean.

They know which way to run, though.

turtle hatchling

Tiny turtles, big enemies

Once they are in the sea, turtle hatchlings swim as fast as they can away from the shore.

The hatchlings are just two inches (5 cm) long.

Many ocean enemies, such as sharks and other large fish, will try to eat them.

The tiny turtles hide in **seaweed** to stay safe.

seaweed

turtle hatchling

The life of a turtle

After about ten years, the young turtles have grown to the size of dinner plates.

They have swum thousands of miles from the beach where they hatched.

They spend their days looking for food, such as ocean plants, jellyfish, crabs, and lobsters.

Their strong mouths are just right for crunching through the shells of the animals they eat.

jellyfish

crab

loggerhead turtle

lobster

A special beach

When a female loggerhead turtle is about 30 years old, she is a fully-grown adult.

Soon, she will swim to the beach where she hatched from her egg—even if it is thousands of miles away.

When she arrives, she will dig a nest and lay her eggs—as her mother once did years before.

adult female loggerhead turtle

Glossary

flippers (FLIP-urz)
body parts, a little
like legs or arms, that
water animals such as
turtles and dolphins
use to help them swim

hatch (HATCH) to
break out of an egg

hatchlings (HACH-lingz) baby animals, such as turtles, that have just hatched from their eggs

nest (NEST) a safe place or home made by an animal where it lays its eggs

seaweed (SEE-weed) living things that grow in oceans and look like plants

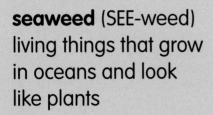

Index

Read more

Hall, Kirsten. *Leatherback Turtle (SuperSized!)*. New York: Bearport Publishing (2007).

Marsh, Laura. *Sea Turtles (National Geographic Readers)*. Washington, D.C.: National Geographic Society (2011).

Wearing, Judy. *Sea Turtles (World of Wonder)*. New York: Weigl Publishers Inc. (2010).

Learn more online

To learn more about sea turtles, visit
www.bearportpublishing.com/WaterBabies

About the author

Ruth Owen has been writing children's books for more than ten years. She particularly enjoys working on books about animals and the natural world. Ruth lives in Cornwall, England, just minutes from the ocean. She loves gardening and caring for her family of llamas.